Haiku History

ALSO BY H.W. BRANDS

T.R.: The Last Romantic (1997)

The First American: The Life and Times of Benjamin Franklin
    (2000)

The Age of Gold: The California Gold Rush and the New American
    Dreams (2002)

Lone Star Nation: How a Ragged Army of Courageous Volunteers
    Won the Battle for Texas Independence (2004)

Andrew Jackson: His Life and Times (2005)

Traitor to His Class: The Privileged Life and Radical Presidency
    of Franklin Delano Roosevelt (2008)

American Colossus: The Triumph of Capitalism, 1865–1900
    (2010)

The Murder of Jim Fisk for the Love of Josie Mansfield (2011)

The Heartbreak of Aaron Burr (2012)

The Man Who Saved the Union: Ulysses Grant in War and Peace
    (2012)

Reagan: The Life (2015)

The General vs. the President: MacArthur and Truman at the
    Brink of Nuclear War (2016)

Heirs of the Founders: The Epic Rivalry of Henry Clay, John
    Calhoun, and Daniel Webster, the Second Generation of
    American Giants (2018)

Dreams of El Dorado: A History of the American West (2019)

Haiku History
The American Saga
Three Lines at a Time

H.W. Brands

University of Texas Press

Austin

Requests for permission to reproduce material from this work
should be sent to:
Permissions
University of Texas Press
P.O. Box 7819
Austin, TX 78713-7819
utpress.utexas.edu/rp-form

♾ The paper used in this book meets the minimum requirements
of ANSI/NISO Z39.48-1992 (R1997) (Permanence of Paper).

Library of Congress Cataloging-in-Publication Data

Names: Brands, H.W., author.
Title: Haiku history : the American saga three lines at a time /
    H.W. Brands.
Description: First edition. | Austin : University of Texas Press,
    2020. Identifiers: LCCN 2019015612
ISBN 978-1-4773-2032-7 (cloth : alk. paper)
ISBN 978-1-4773-2033-4 (library e-book)
ISBN 978-1-4773-2034-1 (non-library e-book)
Subjects: LCSH: Haiku, American. | United States—History—
    Poetry. Classification: LCC PS3552.R32 H35 2020 | DDC
    811./54—dc23
LC record available at https://lccn.loc.gov/2019015612

doi:10.7560/320327

Contents

Preface

This book grew out of a long-running conversation held over breakfast at Sweetish Hill Bakery in Austin, Texas. Greg Curtis, Steve Harrigan, Larry Wright, and I gather weekly to discuss various topics; the fact that we are all writers means that the topics include writing. As audiobooks became increasingly available early in this century, we reflected on whether this would change the way books are written. If most readers were actually listeners, would the visual cues writers employ—paragraphing, for example—lose their force? We considered whether other changes in technology were already affecting the art of storytelling. Would email and text-messaging replace traditional dialogue in novels? Would future historians turn to Facebook to find out what their subjects were thinking and doing? Would tech-shrunk attention spans compel us to write shorter books, or at least shorter chapters?

About this time Twitter burst onto the scene, at the 2007 iteration of the South by Southwest Interactive conference in Austin. I was intrigued. What could anyone say in 140 characters? For years I had been telling my students, when they asked about the word limits I placed on their essays, that the history of the world can be written in 800 words or 8 million words; the only difference is the degree of detail. But 140 characters? I took it as a challenge. Could I write history under such constraints? I didn't propose to write a whole history in one tweet; that would be absurd. But maybe I could do it in a series of tweets.

I had another motive. I have long observed that history is largely lost on the young. I lecture to eighteen-year-old first-year students at the University of Texas; I also lecture to much older men and women in the several continuing-education programs UT operates. And I can say without fear of contradiction that the latter come to class already interested in history, while most of the former have to be enticed. This is unsurprising and as things should be: the young ought to be looking forward, not back.

Even so, it gave me something else to think about as I weighed the effects of changes in technology on the historical enterprise. Twitter was soon the rage, especially among my students. I thought if I reached them where they spent their free time, perhaps I could draw them in.

My reflections took an unexpected twist in one seminar. As I explained to the students how they should format their term papers, I told them that these instructions were recommendations rather than requirements. I said the format had worked well for students in the past, but if they really wanted to devise a format of their own, they could. "Genius makes its own rules," I said. As a throwaway line, I added, "If you want to write your papers in the form of haiku, be my guest."

"Professor Brands," one student responded. "Have you ever written history as haiku?"

A light went on in my head. Even as I conceded that I had not, I asked myself *why* not? I realized that the standard haiku format of seventeen syllables would fit comfortably within the

140-character constraint of a tweet. It would also have the effect of novelty. In the crowded world of social media, people might notice an attempt to write history as a species of short-form poetry.

Thus my project began. I set out to write a history of the United States, one haiku at a time, and to publish it via Twitter. It didn't take me long to discover *why* history had not previously been written—to my knowledge, anyway—as haiku. The haiku is a deliberately static form, often employed to encourage contemplation of a scene in nature. Histories, by contrast, are full of action. The haiku is like a photograph, while histories are films. Epic storytellers of the past employed rhythm schemes that carried the reader along— the dactylic hexameters of Homer, for instance— rather than forcing repeated halts in the action.

But I plunged ahead. And I came to appreciate a fortuitous match between Twitter and haiku. I intended to tweet once every day or two, so poetic momentum would have been lost anyway. And the haiku made *me* stop and contemplate the scenes I was describing. What emotions could I summon to characterize the struggles of the early immigrants to the Americas? What were the reactions of the indigenous peoples to the new arrivals? In the moment before shooting broke the stillness at Lexington on the fateful morning of April 19, 1775, what thoughts were running through the heads of the Massachusetts minutemen and the British redcoats?

I didn't consider ahead of time how long it would take to write my history. I didn't outline the project in advance. Having taught and written American history for more than three decades, I knew the broad story, but I let myself speed up or slow down as the spirit moved me. In the early going I leaped centuries between installments; later, mere months, days or even hours.

It took me several years to reach the twenty-first century. I occasionally thought about gathering the installments and publishing them in print. Some readers encouraged me to do just that, to make them easier to find. I put off deciding until I got so close to the present that I was writing current events rather than history.

Ultimately, I chose to make a book of them. Not all of them, by any means: they numbered many more than a thousand by this time, and I couldn't see inflicting such a quantity on readers, however patient. Again, haiku are intended to be spare, and nothing is spare in such numbers.

So I made a selection, the ones included here. They start millennia ago and run to the current century. Readers will recognize the key events and developments of American history, though most readers will notice omissions, perhaps of some of their favorite events. This is unavoidable, and for it I make no apology. I ask only that readers dip into the book wherever they like, and read in small doses, one or a few haiku at a sitting.

Read, reflect, enjoy.

1 * Origins

Walking from Asia
A hunter, a tribe, a clan
Into a new world.

· *First arrivals, c. 15,000 BC*

The Norsemen sail west
For fish, grapes, a plot of ground
Then sail east again.

· *Newfoundland, c. AD 1000*

The white ships appear
The bearded ones come ashore
Who the hell are they?

· *Columbus, 1492*

Fever takes the young
Their parents weep, then die too
Whole peoples perish.

· *First contacts, 15th–19th centuries*

Gold! There will be gold!
For gentlemen to gather
In fair Virginia!

· *Jamestown's promise, 1607*

No gold, no profit
No corn, no meat, no sugar
Nothing but hunger.

· *Virginia's reality, 1607–1624*

. . . .
. . . .

Torn from their homeland
Transported in misery
To toil in chains.

· *Slave trade, 17th–19th centuries*

A cold churning sea
A windswept peninsula
This is a refuge?

· *Plymouth, 1620*

We solemnly swear
As a joint body to seek
The general good.

· *Mayflower Compact, 1620*

Terror in the night
Blood and slaughter in the day
Horror on the land.

- *King Philip's War, 1670s*

Shivers and specters
Flit over souls in Salem
As nineteen are hanged.

- *Witch trials, 1690s*

New lights and new hearts
New preachers from new pulpits
Awaken the world.

- *Great Awakening, 1730s to 1740s*

Victory burdens
An empire deeply in debt
London retrenches.

· *Aftermath of French and Indian War, 1763*

Taxes, new taxes
That drive a free people to
Arson and riot.

· *Stamp Act protests, 1765*

Taunts and ice balls fly
Nervous soldiers flinch and fire
Blood moon, scarlet snow.

· *Boston Massacre, 1770*

In angry war paint
Men board three Indiamen
And toss the cargo.

· *Boston Tea Party, 1773*

Gruff men, frightened boys
Face off, then fire unknowing
And shatter a world.

· *Battle of Lexington, 1775*

A congress debates
Before a heart-stopping leap
To independence.

· *Declaration of Independence, 1776*

Whigs battle Tories
Fathers take arms against sons
The people divide.

· *The Revolution as civil war, 1775–1783*

Franklin charms Paris
Gates batters Burgoyne, bringing
France into the war.

· *Battle of Saratoga, 1777*

Frozen sky, iron earth
Tattered clothes, empty bellies
Verging on defeat.

· *Valley Forge, 1778*

A hesitant step
Toward a national union
With war as cement.

· *Articles of Confederation, 1781*

French money and ships
American muskets and will
Bring Cornwallis down.

· *Battle of Yorktown, 1781*

A year of wrangling
After six years of fighting
And the deed is done.

· *Treaty of Paris, 1783*

. . . .
. . . .

In victory's warmth
The glue of their common fear
Melts alarmingly.

· *Postwar discontent, 1780s*

America stumbles
On account of selfish states
Behaving badly.

· *Crisis of the 1780s*

Two men of vision
Madison and Hamilton
Quietly plot a coup.

· *Origins of the Constitution, 1786*

Delegates gather
To subvert one government
And craft another.

· *Philadelphia, 1787*

In secret debate
In Philadelphia's heat
The fifty-five wrangle.

· *Constitutional Convention, 1787*

They limit the states
And strengthen central power
To build a nation.

· *Constitutional Convention, 1787*

To secure the South
The drafters knowingly make
A devil's bargain.

· *Slavery in the Constitution, 1787*

They sign the charter
And send it to the people
For their yea or nay.

· *Ratification debate, 1787–1788*

The battle is joined
The Antis cry freedom's doom
But fail to persuade.

· *Constitution ratified, 1787–1788*

2 * The New Nation

At Federal Hall
A federal government
Restarts the republic.

· *George Washington inaugurated, 1789*

The Congress convenes
Its first order of business:
To guarantee rights.

· *Bill of Rights, 1789*

America's flame
Kindles dry forests in France
The heat cracks the earth.

· *French Revolution, 1789*

Amid the conflict
Factions form, parties congeal
Old patriots weep.

· *America's first parties, 1790s*

The Congress threatens
Free speech and encourages
Xenophobia.

· *Alien and Sedition Acts, 1798*

Kentucky resolves
To refuse obedience.
Virginia seconds.

· *Kentucky and Virginia Resolutions, 1798–1799*

Ingenious device
Separates cotton from seeds
Gives bondage new life.

· *Cotton gin, 1793*

The whip still slashes
The chains still burden and bruise
But the ships sail by.

· *Atlantic slave trade to the U.S. ends, 1808*

A Western empire
Suddenly offered for sale:
Louisiana.

· *Louisiana Purchase, 1803*

Up the Missouri
Over the mountains, clear to
The far Pacific.

· *Lewis and Clark expedition, 1804–1806*

Trouble with Europe
Ships and cargoes snatched at sea
By Britain and France.

· *U.S. amid the Napoleonic Wars, 1803–1815*

Jefferson responds
With a blanket embargo
That staggers commerce.

· *Embargo Act, 1807*

New England erupts
Federalists fulminate
All curse Jefferson.

· *Reaction to Embargo Act, 1807 and after*

War feeling rises
Anglophobia rages
Hottest in the West.

· *Approach of the War of 1812*

A dismal conflict
Dashing vainglorious hopes
Embarrassing all.

· *War of 1812*

The Capitol burned
The government driven off
The war hawks chastened.

· *War of 1812*

Comes almost too late
The war's singular hero
Stout Old Hickory.

· *Andrew Jackson, 1814–1815*

He smites the British
At the gates of New Orleans
Salvaging honor.

· *Jackson in the Battle of New Orleans, 1815*

Jackson rides farther:
Into Spanish Florida
And Madrid gives way.

· *Acquisition of Florida, 1819*

Indians also
Get thrust aside by Jackson
Whom they call Sharp Knife.

· *Indian removal, 1810s to 1830s*

Missouri's entrance
Draws a line on slavery
And provokes alarm.

· *Missouri Compromise, 1820*

"A corrupt bargain!"
The Jacksonians bellow
And plot their revenge.

· *Reaction to election of 1824*

Though Jackson prevails
Wife Rachel, slandered, libeled
Collapses and dies.

· *Election of 1828*

Jackson despairing
Yet travels to Washington
To take his next post.

· *Jackson's inauguration, 1829*

Thousands go with him
Delirious, triumphant
The people will rule!

· *Jackson's inauguration, 1829*

Trouble in Charleston
Murmurings of secession
Over a tariff.

· *Nullification crisis, 1828–1833*

I'll hang the traitors
High as Haman! Every one!
The Union shall stand!

· *Jackson against South Carolina, 1832–1833*

Carolina heeds
Old Hickory's warnings
The crisis passes.

· *Compromise of 1833*

A new foe springs up
The haughty and powerful
Nicholas Biddle.

· *"Bank War," 1832–33*

Jackson undaunted
Strikes at brazen Biddle
In his marble lair.

· *Jackson and the Bank War, 1833*

He strangles the Bank
By withdrawing deposits
That Biddle requires.

· *Jackson and the Bank War, 1833*

A thousand wagons
Cross the muddy Missouri
Ho for Oregon!

· *Westward migration, 1843*

James Polk grows greedy
Coveting California
He provokes a war.

· *War with Mexico, 1846*

The bluecoats attack
Taking Mexico City
Forcing surrender.

· *War with Mexico, 1846–1848*

A glint, a glimmer
In the dawn, in the millrace
A fateful yellow.

· *Gold in California, 1848*

The argonauts come
Drawn by invisible threads
The heartstrings of hope.

· *California gold rush, 1849*

....
....

They demand a state
And write a constitution
Which they forward east.

· *California applies for admission, 1850*

It lands like a bomb
In a tense, riven Congress
Washington shudders.

· *California crisis, 1850*

Anxious defusers
Approach it delicately
Seeking solution.

· *California crisis, 1850*

The nation trembles
The Union hangs in balance . . .
At last, an answer.

· *Compromise of 1850*

3 * Union on Trial

But powder has spilled
And bits of fuse still smolder
The danger persists.

· *Aftermath of Compromise of 1850*

Arrives a firebrand
The gaunt monomaniac
Ohio's John Brown.

· *Kansas, 1856*

His band of zealots
Gird with swords and the Bible
To smite the slave-men.

· *Pottawatomie massacre, 1856*

The killings appall
But then fade into others
On that bloody ground.

· *Kansas, 1856*

Enter the black robes
The eminent justices
To join the struggle.

· *Dred Scott case, 1857*

Congress, they say
Has no power to prevent
Slavery's wide spread.

· *Dred Scott case, 1857*

John Brown once again
Hears heaven's call to take arms
And slay the wicked.

· *Raid on Harpers Ferry, 1859*

No mere murders now
But a full-blown rebellion
In slavery's heart.

· *Harpers Ferry, 1859*

The enterprise fails
Brown is wounded, captured, tried
Condemned to be hanged.

· *Harpers Ferry, 1859*

Evil terrorist!
Says the South; but in the North:
Hail to the martyr!

· *Reactions to John Brown, 1859*

Balloting divides
The nation as ne'er before
Dark horse Lincoln wins.

· *Election of 1860*

The South takes alarm
Seven states caucus, decide
To leave the Union.

· *Secession, 1860–1861*

What will Lincoln do?
'Tis the question of the hour
Will he yield or fight?

· *Lincoln and secession, 1861*

He dispatches supplies
To a besieged, outgunned fort
In Charleston's harbor.

· *Faceoff at Fort Sumter, April 1861*

Invasion! declare
The seceders, who train guns
On the fort and fire.

· *Shelling of Fort Sumter, April 1861*

Thus begins the war
Of brother against brother
State against Union.

- *Start of the Civil War, April 1861*

Lincoln calls for troops
Brave men to uphold the law
And save the Union.

- *Lincoln summons volunteers, April 1861*

Toward Manassas
The Federals march, flags high
And spirits higher.

- *Battle of Bull Run, Virginia, July 1861*

The Virginians reel
The Federals celebrate
Their expected win.

· *Battle of Bull Run, July 1861*

Too soon, though, too soon!
For the Virginians regroup
And carry the day.

· *Battle of Bull Run, July 1861*

Away in the West
Where the great rivers mingle
Green Grant learns to lead.

· *Ulysses S. Grant, autumn 1861*

Attack and attack!
Is his motto and ethic
Strike and strike again!

· *Grant to Shiloh, spring 1862*

But now the striker
Is caught off balance, surprised
And soon retreating.

· *Shiloh, April 1862*

Yet Sherman holds firm
Trading his inner demons
For rebel devils.

· *William T. Sherman at Shiloh, April 1862*

The second day dawns
The bluecoats counterattack
And scatter the foe.

· *Shiloh, April 1862*

Grant is applauded
For the victory—but oh
The terrible cost!

· *Aftermath of Shiloh, 1862*

Lee and the rebels
Cross the Potomac and bring
The war to the North.

· *Robert E. Lee in Maryland, September 1862*

The bluecoats attack
Charging, firing, hurrahing
For cause and country!

· *Antietam, September 1862*

The rebels recoil
Then counterattack screaming
Blood drenches the ground.

· *Antietam, September 1862*

The bodies mount high
The agony continues
Till night brings a halt.

· *Antietam, September 1862*

Lee counts his losses
And changes his strategy
He withdraws toward home.

· *After Antietam, 1862*

Lincoln sees his chance
To make freedom a war aim
Against the rebels.

· *Preliminary Emancipation*
Proclamation, September 1862

The Union's gunboats
Command the Mississippi
Except near Vicksburg.

· *Vicksburg campaign, 1863*

Grant invests the town
He lobs shells over its walls
The siege takes a toll.

· *Vicksburg, early summer 1863*

A white flag goes up!
The Confederates march out
The city is Grant's.

· *Surrender of Vicksburg, July 1863*

Lincoln hails the word
The great river again flows
Unvex'd to the sea.

· *Response to Vicksburg, July 1863*

Lee's soldiers need food
Virginia's larders are bare
Her fields exhausted.

· *Gettysburg campaign, June–July 1863*

Maryland is lush
Pennsylvania is plenty
Rebel mouths water.

· *Gettysburg campaign, June–July 1863*

Over Potomac
The Confederate troops go
Proud, tough, confident.

· *Gettysburg campaign, June–July 1863*

For two days they fight
To a murderous standoff
With stubborn bluecoats.

· *Gettysburg, July 1863*

Pickett's men gather
Knowing they carry the hope
Of the Southern cause.

· *Gettysburg, third day, July 1863*

Over open fields
They march, into a cyclone
Of noise, shot and shell.

· *Pickett's charge, July 3, 1863*

They fall like ninepins
Yet the others keep marching
Toward the Union ridge.

· *Pickett's charge, July 3, 1863*

But they are too few
They stagger and fall; with them
Fade the rebel hopes.

· *Confederate defeat at Gettysburg, July 1863*

In the South, Sherman
Cunningly takes Atlanta
And heads for the sea.

· *Sherman's march, late 1864*

His bummers range far
Raiding barns, sheds and houses
Stripping the region.

· *Sherman's march, late 1864*

Meanwhile Grant tightens
A noose around Lee's army
Besieged at Richmond.

· *Final phase of the war, early 1865*

Lee, nearly hopeless
At length abandons Richmond
To give Grant the slip.

· *Virginia campaign, early 1865*

But Phil Sheridan
Cuts him off, ending the war
At Appomattox.

· *Lee's surrender, April 1865*

Lincoln, gratified
Relaxes for the first time
In four wearing years.

· *Ford's Theater, April 1865*

John Wilkes Booth gets word
Of the Lincolns' attendance
And loads his pistol.

· *Assassination of Lincoln, April 1865*

4 * Into the Modern

The war freed the slaves
Without humbling their masters
Who aim to recoup.

· *Aftermath of emancipation, 1865–*

Black codes reproduce
Slavery under new guise
The freedmen aren't free.

· *Reconstruction, 1865–1866*

With flame, lead and rope
Nightriders broadcast terror
To restore the old.

· *Ku Klux Klan in the South, late 1860s*

But Grant steps forward
Sends soldiers against the Klan
And breaks its power.

· *President Grant defeats the KKK, 1871*

Yet violence persists
The fact and the threat color
Blacks' everyday lives.

· *The South, late 1800s*

They toil as tenants
For a slim share of the crop
Forever cotton.

· *Southern sharecroppers, late 1800s*

Whites have it hard too
For the South is money-poor
And slow to evolve.

· *The South, late 1800s*

The North meanwhile booms
And then busts, and booms again
Manic to panic.

· *Gilded Age economy, late 1800s*

One panic afflicts
Markets in every city
America reels.

· *Panic of 1873*

Prices fall for goods
Of factory, mine and farm
Demand disappears.

· *Panic of 1873*

Mill owners shutter
Their works, laying off thousands
And then thousands more.

· *Depression of 1870s*

Workers wander dazed
Muttering, moaning, cursing
What is to be done?

· *Depression of 1870s*

Railroad men link arms
In grim solidarity
Against the bosses.

- *Great Railroad Strike, 1877*

A fair wage, they ask
To feed our wives and children
Who shiver and cry.

- *Great Railroad Strike, 1877*

Anarchy! Murder!
Thunder the powers that be
A red tide rises!

- *Great Railroad Strike, 1877*

America cheers
As federal troops roll in
And smash the strikers.

· *Great Railroad Strike, 1877*

Far off in the West
The ultimate vanquishing
Begins to unfold.

· *War for the Plains, 1870s*

After decades struggling
One tribe after another
Is compelled to yield.

· *War for the Plains, 1870s*

But small bands resist
Crazy Horse and Sitting Bull
Defy the bluecoats.

· *Little Bighorn, 1876*

Golden-Hair charges
He sees only victory
And glory this day.

· *Custer at Little Bighorn, 1876*

But his prize is death
Crazy Horse has set a trap
And Custer falls in.

· *Little Bighorn, 1876*

Sioux warriors stay strong
But the women and children
Lack food and fall sick.

· *After Little Bighorn, late 1870s*

Exhausted, the Sioux
Surrender, yielding to fate
And too many whites.

· *After Little Bighorn, late 1870s*

But some hear a call
To raise the spirits again
By sacred dancing.

· *To Wounded Knee, 1880s to 1890*

The soldiers take fright
They say the dancing must stop
And dancers disperse.

· *Wounded Knee, 1890*

A shot, and more shots
Then a tempest of gunfire
Blasts the Sioux tepees.

· *Wounded Knee, 1890*

Many scores slaughtered
Men, women, children, old, young
Lie dead in the snow.

· *Wounded Knee, 1890*

On Erie's south shore
Grows up a pious young man
With killer instincts.

· *John D. Rockefeller, 1850s*

Into oil—black gold!
He ventures, and discovers
His special genius.

· *Rockefeller, 1870s*

His company grows
The Standard Oil behemoth
A law to itself.

· *Rockefeller and Standard Oil, 1880s*

Elsewhere arises
Another titan, of steel
Andrew Carnegie.

· *Carnegie and steel, 1880s to 1890s*

At Homestead he builds
A magnificent new plant
Envy of the world.

· *Carnegie and steel, 1890s*

He drives his costs down
For ore, for coal and transport
For human labor.

· *Carnegie and Homestead strike, 1892*

Mute ore cannot bleed
Nor coal grow weak and hungry
But living men do.

· *Homestead strike, 1892*

They form a union
To guard their rights and their pay
From Carnegie's cuts.

· *Homestead strike, 1892*

Carnegie's soldiers
Pinkerton mercenaries
Browbeat the union.

· *Homestead strike, 1892*

The union fights back
With fists, bullets and firebombs
A river runs red.

- *Homestead strike, 1892*

The greatest mogul
Is less wealthy but more shrewd
Jupiter Morgan.

- *Rise of J. P. Morgan, 1880s*

Master of money
And with money, connections
That produce great power.

- *Morgan, 1880s*

When railroads panic
Morgan throws them a lifeline
Which becomes a noose.

· *Morgan, 1880s to 1890s*

In time Uncle Sam
Amid the worst panic yet
Must turn to Morgan.

· *Morgan bails out the Treasury, 1895*

He lays out his terms
Gold, he offers; gold for bonds
Gold or certain ruin.

· *Morgan and Grover Cleveland, 1895*

Cleveland, reluctant
Silences his principles
And takes Morgan's gold.

· *Morgan's syndicate, 1895*

Wall Street breathes again
And hails Morgan as hero
The savior of all!

· *Morgan's gold deal, 1895*

But others decry
One man's wielding such power
Is freedom finished?

· *Backlash after Morgan's gold deal, 1895*

Bryan damns Morgan
For crucifying mankind
On a cross of gold!

· *William Jennings Bryan at the Democratic
convention, 1896*

His campaign rages
Across the land, stirring hopes
Summoning dark fears.

· *Bryan vs. William McKinley, 1896*

Bryan, tired and hoarse
Battles bravely to the end
Only to be trounced.

· *McKinley victory, 1896*

5 * A World before Them

A brutal conflict
In nearby Spanish Cuba
Touches many hearts.

· *Road to war with Spain, 1895–1898*

McKinley resists
American involvement
He doesn't want war.

· *To the Spanish-American War, 1897–1898*

But war sells papers
It lets young men be heroes
And nations feel strong.

· *To the Spanish-American War, 1897–1898*

A soft Cuban night
Is appallingly shattered
A great explosion!

· *Destruction of the* Maine, *1898*

Once joined, the conflict
Proceeds to a swift triumph
For America.

· *Spanish-American War, 1898*

And the victory
Refashions the republic
Into an empire.

· *Annexation of Philippines and
Puerto Rico, 1899*

Then an anarchist
Makes one of the war heroes
The next president.

· *McKinley assassinated; Theodore Roosevelt
  enters the White House, 1901*

Rough Riding TR
Takes on Jupiter Morgan
Haughty as ever.

· *Roosevelt vs. Morgan, 1901*

The attack succeeds
Morgan is forced to disgorge
TR struts proudly.

· *Roosevelt breaks up Northern
  Securities, 1902–1904*

To build a canal
TR makes revolution
In Colombia.

· *TR and Panama, 1903*

The rebels repay
With a slice of their booty
TR starts digging.

· *TR and the Panama Canal, 1903–1904*

To rescue farmers
He fashions novel restraints
On railroad charges.

· *TR and regulation of railroads, 1902–1906*

To save ancient trees
He waves his pen and voilà!
New forest reserves.

· *TR and conservation, 1906–1909*

To ensure pure food
He cleans up slaughterhouses
With muckrakers' help.

· *TR and consumer safety, 1906–1909*

His time running out
He anoints a successor
Sweet-hearted Bill Taft.

· *TR and William Howard Taft, 1908*

Still itching to fight
TR heads to Africa
To battle lions.

· *TR on safari, 1909*

J. P. Morgan cheers
And celebrates with a toast:
"Luck to the lions!"

· *TR sails away, 1909*

Before long Big Bill
Reveals the unexpected:
A mind of his own.

· *TR and Taft, 1910–1912*

Roosevelt bridles
He claims he has been betrayed
He challenges Taft.

· *TR vs. Taft, 1912*

TR's defection
Cripples Taft, but the winner
Is Woodrow Wilson.

· *Election of 1912*

Professor Wilson
An unlikely president
Stern yet eloquent.

· *Wilson takes office, 1913*

HAIKU HISTORY

. . . .
. . . .

He follows TR
And Taft in chastising wealth
And excess power.

· *Wilson as president, 1913–1914*

When Europe erupts
He declares neutrality
In thought, word and deed.

· *Wilson's response to war in Europe, 1914*

But profit beckons
America's money men
When Europe needs loans.

· *Wartime finance, 1914–1915*

The bankers demand
That the president let them
Underwrite the war.

· *Wartime finance, 1914–1915*

At length he approves
The money shall flow to all
Who can pay for it.

· *Wilson allows loans to the belligerents, 1915*

Slowly but surely
Neutrality wears thinner
The pull of war grows.

· *America moves toward war, 1916*

German submarines
The stealthy, deadly U-boats
Claim their fateful toll.

· *American ships torpedoed, 1917*

Neutral no longer
Wilson gets Congress to vote
In favor of war.

· *America goes to war, 1917*

Off sail the doughboys
To fill the trenches of France
And battle the Hun.

· *American troops in World War I, 1917–1918*

Their arrival cheers
The French and British, who mount
A great offensive.

· *World War I, 1917–1918*

The Germans stagger
They weaken and finally
Sign an armistice.

· *End of World War I, November 1918*

Attention adjourns
To Paris, where peacemakers
Gather and argue.

· *Paris Peace Conference, 1919*

Wilson the righteous
Eschews national interest
For a grand vision.

· *Wilson in Paris, 1919*

A League of Nations
World government by the good
To awe wrongdoers.

· *Wilson and the Treaty of Versailles, 1919*

At the Senate door
Stands glowering Cabot Lodge
To block Wilson's way.

· *Henry Cabot Lodge against the treaty, 1919*

Wilson stumps the land
Preaching national glory
In the fight for right.

· *Wilson for the treaty, 1919*

His words sing and soar
They mesmerize and convince
The people rally.

· *Wilson for the treaty, 1919*

And then, all at once
The thrilling words are cut off
Wilson falls silent.

· *Wilson's stroke, 1919*

With no champion
The treaty dies at the hands
Of the smirking Lodge.

· *Senate rejects Treaty of Versailles,*
1919–1920

6 * Rendezvous
with Destiny

RENDEZVOUS WITH DESTINY

. . . .
. . . .

The mood in the land
Grows ugly and contentious
For what did we fight?

· *Questioning of World War I, 1919*

A bomb detonates
One night on a leafy street
Close to the White House.

· *Attempted assassination of*
A. Mitchell Palmer, 1919

Palmer, spared, reacts
He dispatches his agents
To round up the reds.

· *Red Scare, 1919–1920*

Tolerance withers
Nativism resurges
In hoods and white robes.

· *New Ku Klux Klan, 1910s to 1920s*

From the Christian right
Comes an attack on Darwin
And evolution.

· *Scopes trial, 1925*

The country goes dry
But not gladly or as one
Cities want their booze.

· *Prohibition, 1920s*

Bootleggers oblige
Beer and liquor flow freely
For those in the know.

· *Speakeasy culture, 1920s*

Profits, too, flow strong
In the canyons of Wall Street
Shares frothily surge.

· *Stock market, 1920s*

Investors pile in
Butchers, bakers and even
Candlestick makers.

· *Stock market, 1920s*

But the good times end
With a shriek and a shudder
One savage Tuesday.

· *Stock market crash, 1929*

The stock crash engulfs
The banks; their reserves vanish
As though by armed theft.

· *Great Crash, 1929*

Workers lose their jobs
Their paychecks, their homes, their pride
And lastly their hope.

· *Bank panic, early 1930s*

The homeless wander
The streets, the roads, the highways
The trains to nowhere.

· *Great Depression, 1930s*

Some protest, some march
An army of haggard vets
Heads for Washington.

· *Bonus Army, 1932*

Douglas MacArthur
Chief of staff, sends a column
To scatter the vets.

· *Bonus Army, 1932*

Franklin Roosevelt
Shakes his head and tells a friend
"This will elect me."

· *Rise of FDR, 1932*

He enters office
Asserting nothing to fear
Naught but fear itself.

· *FDR's inauguration, 1933*

He summons Congress
To emergency session
To rescue the banks.

· *FDR and the New Deal, 1933*

He sends more measures
To Congress, which passes them
With record swiftness.

• *Hundred Days, 1933*

Relief for the poor
Jobs for the willing jobless
Price help for farmers.

• *Hundred Days, 1933*

The nation's head spins
Is it too much? Too little?
Too stingy? Too dear?

• *Hundred Days, 1933*

Hope slowly revives
In some circles; in others
Resentment takes root.

· *Reaction to the New Deal, 1933*

Trouble overseas
Looms large: Europe and Asia
Convulse with violence.

· *Rise of fascism, 1930s*

Japan rapes China
Hitler brutalizes Jews
Innocence succumbs.

· *Rise of fascism, 1930s*

Roosevelt, cautious
Gently warns of disaster
The nation still sleeps.

· *American isolationism, 1930s*

Japan runs rampant
Hitler grows bolder each month
A new war begins.

· *Coming of World War II, 1939*

America arms
And aids Britain and China
But stays clear itself.

· *World War II, 1939–1941*

Till war comes at last
From a blue Pacific sky
One Sunday morning.

· *Pearl Harbor, Dec. 7, 1941*

The nation unites
Enemies have that effect
In unity, strength.

· *America at war, 1941–1945*

Industry churns out
Planes, tanks, trucks, ships, bombs, boots, guns
As never before.

· *Arsenal America, 1941–1945*

Armadas sail east
Armadas sail west, seeking
A place to engage.

· *America at war, 1941–1945*

First blood in the west
At Coral Sea and Midway
Japan is turned back.

· *War in the Pacific, 1942*

In North Africa
A landing, a field to fight
The Nazi machine.

· *Invasion of North Africa, 1942*

From North Africa
To Italy, the fighting
Engulfs a new land.

· *War in Southern Europe, 1943*

More troops are gathered
Boats and ships by the thousand
For fateful D-Day.

· *Invasion of France, 1944*

The assault force sails
Its artillery thunders
At the German wall.

· *D-Day, June 6, 1944*

Soaking and deafened
GIs storm the beach to seize
A bloody foothold.

- *D-Day, June 6, 1944*

To the east they march
Rolling back the Nazi tide
And freeing Paris.

- *Liberation of France, 1944*

On east to the Rhine
For the fatal final stroke
At Hitler's black heart.

- *Last days of the Third Reich, 1945*

The monster is slain
But his fell allies persist
In the Pacific.

· *Final phase of the war against Japan, 1945*

Such bitter fighting
No Americans have seen
War to the last man.

· *Okinawa, 1945*

Harry S Truman
Warns of annihilation
If Japan fights on.

· *Last days of the war, 1945*

A secret weapon
Harnessing the universe
Rests in Truman's hands.

· *Atom bomb, 1945*

He gives the order:
End the present agony
Unleash the atom.

· *Hiroshima, Nagasaki, and Japan's*
surrender, 1945

7 * Bestride the Planet

In victory's sigh
Commences a new struggle
A strangely cold war.

- *U.S. vs. Soviet Union, 1945 and after*

Real fighting erupts
In divided Korea
The Cold War grows hot.

- *Korean War, 1950–1953*

Amid the conflict
Something historic occurs
Blacks fight next to whites.

- *Integration of the military, early 1950s*

On civilian fronts
The cause of equality
Moves forward by steps.

· *Civil rights movement, 1950s*

The nation's high court
Undoes decades and expels
Jim Crow from the schools.

· Brown v. Board of Education, *1954*

Footsore Rosa Parks
Declares, "Enough!" and rejects
The back of the bus.

· *Montgomery bus boycott, 1955*

A young minister
Able and charismatic
Is thrust to the fore.

· *Emergence of Martin Luther King, 1955–1956*

Momentum gathers
For the biggest protest yet
On the nation's mall.

· *March on Washington, 1963*

Hundreds of thousands
Blacks and some whites, young and old
Come to Washington.

· *March on Washington, 1963*

To one above all
They listen most intently
Martin Luther King.

· *March on Washington, 1963*

He speaks of a dream
When one's color won't matter
When freedom will ring.

· *King at the Lincoln Memorial, 1963*

The young president
Is murdered; an older one
Takes up the challenge.

· *Lyndon Johnson succeeds John Kennedy, 1963*

In Kennedy's name
He says, and for the nation
We shall overcome.

· *LBJ and civil rights, 1964*

The deadlock gives way
The historic bill is passed
Jim Crow is no more.

· *Civil Rights Act of 1964*

Americans march
Elsewhere that season, far off
In Southeast Asia.

· *Roots of the Vietnam War, early 1960s*

A war with deep roots
And deeper complexities
Grows ever deeper.

· *Vietnam War, 1960s*

What will the world think?
What will Americans say?
If I lose this war?

· *LBJ on Vietnam, 1965*

The war is transformed
It was Vietnam's but now
Is America's.

· *Vietnam War, late 1960s*

Yet for all the troops
And despite all the bombing
The fighting drags on.

· *Vietnam War, late 1960s*

Johnson loses heart
Calls for negotiations
And stops the bombing.

· *Vietnam War, 1968*

Nixon takes over
Draws down American troops
But widens the war.

· *Nixon and Vietnam, 1970*

Yet Hanoi won't yield
Sensing victory nigh in
U.S. exhaustion.

- *Nearing the end in Vietnam, 1972*

America's war
Ends with a shaky peace deal
That no one believes.

- *Paris Peace Accords, 1973*

Dick Nixon meantime
Faces intense scrutiny
Of growing scandal.

- *Watergate, 1973–1974*

A probe discovers
White House tapes—the smoking gun!
But Nixon holds tight.

· *Watergate, 1973–1974*

The case goes to court
The Supremes ponder, then rule
The tapes must be heard.

· *Watergate, 1974*

Their tale is damning
The House moves toward impeachment
Nixon surrenders.

· *Nixon resigns, 1974*

In California
Appears a faded film star
Turned politician.

· *Ronald Reagan, late 1970s*

Fear not, he preaches
America's best days lie
Ahead, not behind.

· *Reagan for president, 1980*

Elected, Reagan
Delivers the coup de grâce
To liberal dreams.

· *Reagan's inauguration, 1981*

Government is not
The solution, he declares
It is the problem.

· *Reagan's inauguration, 1981*

He slashes taxes
To conservatives' delight
Starve the bloated beast!

· *Reagan tax cuts, 1981*

The budget bleeds red
The deficit skyrockets
Some Reaganomics!

· *Reagan deficits, 1980s*

And then a stumble
Reports of a murky scheme
Arms for hostages.

- *Iran-Contra affair, mid-1980s*

Reagan denies it
Until his tale falls apart
The Gipper caught out.

- *Iran-Contra scandal, 1986*

He goes to Berlin
Stands before the hated wall
Throws down a challenge.

- *"Mr. Gorbachev, tear down this wall!" speech, 1987*

Gorbachev chortles
A movie stunt he calls it
The wall doesn't budge.

· *Divided Germany, 1987–1988*

But the ground softens
Ron and Mikhail converse
Improbable friends.

· *Reagan and Gorbachev, 1987–1988*

8 * Vexed Victory

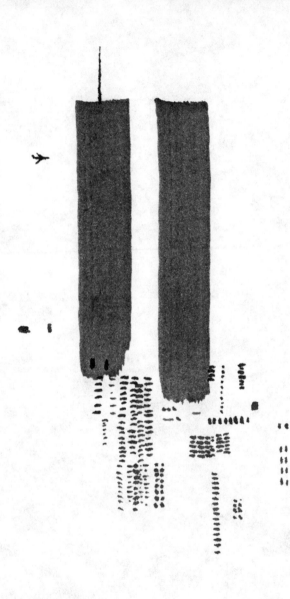

Amid the orchards
Of Santa Clara's valley
A new crop ripens.

· *Silicon Valley, 1970s to 1980s*

Transistors that shrink
And diminish still further
Packed hordes on a chip.

· *Silicon Valley, 1970s to 1980s*

Computers on desks
One to a person rather
Than one to a firm.

· *Personal computer revolution, 1980s*

And soon connected
Form a digital village
A nation, a world.

· *Early Internet, 1980s to 1990s*

Business goes online
Dot-coms here, there, everywhere
A great new gold rush.

· *Dot-com boom, late 1990s*

Odd names, strange concepts
Google, Amazon, Facebook
iPod and iPhone.

· *Tech, early 2000s*

Another turning
Less techie but more profound
Remodels Europe.

· *End of the Cold War, 1989–1991*

Berlin's wall crumbles
Freedom dances on its dust
Germany unites.

· *End of the Cold War, 1989–1991*

The gray empire too
Bereft of belief and nerve
Falls into pieces.

· *Breakup of the Soviet Union, 1991*

HAIKU HISTORY

. . . .
. . . .

Reagan's chosen heir
Eschews triumphalism
Unlike the Gipper.

· *George Bush downplays Cold War victory, 1991*

Bush has fresh problems
Small Kuwait is invaded
By thuggish Saddam.

· *Iraq occupies Kuwait, 1990*

Bush gathers allies
And the UN to assert
A new world order.

· *Bush and the Persian Gulf, 1990–1991*

Five weeks of bombing
Five days of fighting aground
Saddam is beaten.

· *Kuwait liberated, 1991*

But Bush comes up short
Amid a three-way campaign
For reelection.

· *Bill Clinton elected, 1992*

Clinton proposes
A bold health care remedy
Medicare for all.

· *Plan for health care reform, 1993*

The plan is waylaid
By medical lobbyists
And private skeptics.

· *Clinton's failed health care reform, 1993*

Red elephants roar
They trample the blue donkeys
A Newt takes command.

· *Newt Gingrich and Republicans seize House, 1994*

Clinton is cornered
Impeached and put on trial
For bad behavior.

· *Paula Jones and Monica Lewinsky
scandals, 1997–1999*

Shocked, shocked! says the House
Not about the sex—oh no!
Rather, the lying.

· *Clinton impeachment, 1998–1999*

The public differs
Clinton in the Senate dock
Grows more popular.

· *Clinton impeachment fails, 1999*

A presidency
Modestly started is stunned
On a fateful day.

· *George W. Bush, September 11, 2001*

Hijacked airliners
Like manned cruise-missiles target
New York and DC.

· *Terrorist attacks of 9/11*

George W. blinks
Then gathers his wits and nerve
And bullhorns the world.

· *Bush on the rubble of Twin Towers, 2001*

America stands
Says he, and it will commence
A war on terror.

· *Bush after 9/11*

First country attacked:
Afghanistan, training ground
Of bloody Qaeda.

· *U.S. invasion of Afghanistan, 2001*

Second invasion:
Iraq, where Saddam is still
In troubling control.

· *U.S. invades Iraq, 2003*

Deceptively swift
The invasion rolls forward
Saddam is routed.

· *U.S. in Iraq, 2003*

But resistance mounts
The war is just beginning
And drags on and on.

· *Iraq, 2003 and after*

Meanwhile a frenzy
In real estate spreads the wealth
At least on paper.

· *Real estate bubble, 2000–2006*

Like every bubble
This one bursts, and it flattens
The houses of cards.

· *Financial crisis, 2007–2009*

• •
• •

Investors' bad luck
Proves Obama's sudden chance
He slips past McCain.

· *Barack Obama defeats John McCain, 2008*

But what has he won?
The omens are the grimmest
In long memory.

· *Recession, 2009 and after*

Jobless rates rocket
Confidence evaporates
Is there no bottom?

· *Recession 2009–2010*

Slowly and slowly
The listing ship comes aright
The tempest abates.

· *Recovery begins, 2010*

What defied Clinton
Obama accomplishes
Big health care reform.

· *Affordable Care Act, 2010*

Historic and yet
Bitterly controversial
A party-line vote.

· *Affordable Care Act, 2010*

An angry groundswell
Produces a fresh revolt
A new Tea Party.

· *Republican insurgents, 2010*

The lower house flips
The Tea Party commences
Its siege of Barack.

· *Republicans in opposition, 2011*

And early begins
A bruising, bizarre campaign
To take the White House.

· *Donald Trump for president, 2015–2016*

Astonishingly
The utterly unforeseen
Occurs: Trump is prez!

· *Election of 2016*

Artwork by Lauren Nassef

Typeset in Harriet, designed by
Jackson Cavanaugh, Okay Type

Design and composition by
Matt Avery, Monograph